Scattered Reflections

By Jim Ross

Scriptline Images
Beret Imprint
21740 El Puma Cir
Sonora, CA

Copyright © 2016 by Jim Ross. All rights reserved. Printed in the United States of America. No part of this book may be used or reproduced in any manner whatsoever without written permission except in the case of brief quotations embodied in critical articles and reviews. For information address Scriptline Images, 21740 El Puma Circle, Sonora, CA 95370.

Library of Congress Cataloging-in-
Publication Data Ross, Jim (James Lee),
1941--
Scattered Reflections: poetry

Includes bibliographical references and index.
ISBN: 978-0-9978003-0-2
1. poetry. 2. Rhyme.
xxx.x'x—dcxx

ASIN: B01I7JXIF4

Contents

Dedication	5
Victory	6
Part I	**7**
SOME RHYME	**7**
The Wind Plays Well Today	8
Yin Leaves Me	9
Yang Displays His Gold	9
There Goes My Hat	9
The Physician	10
Shipshape and Named	10
Winding Down	10
Desk Rider	12
Passage	12
Last Stroll	13
For Ambrose	13
Purity and Worth	14
Tickle Time	14
Part II	**15**
MORE REASON	**15**
The Tavern of My Delight Serves No Beer	16
Muffin Trouble	17

The Look of Oak	17
Summer Deal	17
Gray as Gloaming in Winter	18
Missouri Tiger Lily Time	18
Good Company	19
The Other Stuff	19
Hold My Hand	22
Questions, Questions	23

Part III — 24
MOSTLY LOVE — 24

The Stuff of Us	25
Time Travel: A Western Solution	26
The Magic West of Home	26
Snap, Crackle, Pique	27
Maggie's Trip	28
Prayer on the Wind	29
Fusion	30
Blink	30
Flights of Fancy	31
My Place or Yours	32
Distortion	32
The Actor	32
Moonless Muse	33

Index of First Lines — 34

Dedication

To the love of my life, Ginny, whose radiance gives me oh-so-needed support, and with a patience *non-pareil*.

Victory

*L*ife with its gains,
cuts in places that leave scars—
where I've bled, I've lived.

Part I
SOME RHYME

The Wind Plays Well Today

*F*irst, the wind discovers chimes
suspended from a tree,
puffs some tiny tickles there
to peal tranquility

For ears that listen anxiously
in golden morning light,
to endless melodies composed
in breezy, playful bites—

The dog next door is also struck
by that which fills the air;
his canine sense knows when to sing
so brings his voice to bear.

Breaths on resin-scented air
discover wood supplies
cathedral ambience for all,
the chimes, the dog, the tree sighs.

I scramble to record the sphere
as gentle shadows wave,
in windblown glory words now spread
across the dappled page.

Suddenly the wind abates,
the flourishes are hushed;
the ink dries at *finale,*
the hillside silent, brushed.

Yin Leaves Me

I shiver when the moon sets,
with the cold fire of desire:
beneath thick covers, beset,
I shiver when the moon sets,
touch loving hands in duet,
building love's consuming pyre,
I shiver when the moon sets,
with the cold fire of desire.

Yang Displays His Gold

*H*e peeks at me, the golden eye, and grins,
light spreading wide as shadows run and hide,
he watches fields as newborn day begins,
he peeks at me, the golden eye, and grins!
He pushes high so heated air begins
to make me sweat great droplets, streaming wide;
he peeks at me, the golden eye, and grins,
light spreading wide as shadows run and hide.

There Goes My Hat

*T*he wind rustles trusting leaves to taunt me,
its sometimes hatted foe, that I'm fair game
for hide-and-seek between twin rows of trees.
The wind rustles trusting leaves to taunt me,
its only rule—that it will change with glee.
It does and claims my hat while I declaim—
the wind rustles trusting leaves to
taunt me— its sometimes hatted foe,
that I'm fair game.

The Physician

*H*is eyes reveal, concern is real,
his hands applied, one knows
care has come and we will heal;
his eyes reveal, concern is real,
our hearts beat still
without appeal. No need,
we see as he bestows—
his eyes reveal, concern
is real,
his hands applied…one knows.

Shipshape and Named

*D*ad looks hard to find his wooden mallet
to rabbet the dead-flat planks, just right.
He'll tap the joints when he can find it—
dad looks hard to find his wooden mallet.
He'll also sculpt a fancy oak-plank billet,
to cite the boat's fine name and birthright—
dad looks hard to find his wooden mallet
to rabbet the dead-flat planks, just right!

Winding Down

*T*he coffee percolated
in a blue enameled pot,
in the darkness of the night
over coals that glowed red hot.

We sat in flitting shadows
swapping tales about the drive

that lay three days behind us—
memories fresh and so alive!

We laughed with Bob's fine version,
how his loop snagged live sagebrush;
the heifer lit for elsewhere
while he cleared the sticky stuff.

Mack poured some steaming coffee
to assuage Bob's empty cup.
*You can chide me all you want,
boys, I've seen your goofs close up!*

We spoke them clear and bold
As the coffee swirls jerked,
one by one we chafed and learned,
the others' little quirks.

How Jill launched Mack to flight
when he put her off her stride—
Mack rolled and lost his jeans
and heard her thump beside his pride.

She's a good old mare, Mack tried,
and *the fault's all mine, you know.
I gotta be more careful, lads
or next time more might show!*

*What about Earl's night fight
with tiny Pine Tree Gray?
The squirrel champ?* laughed Gramp.
*First big cone from that there mug
drops him in the damp!*

With three days sweat behind us,
three more grueling ones to go,
the gab fest winds to silence
as a wind begins to blow.

I came to camp slow riding

from my past—that is, today, sore
to get my mind collected
with these friends…
whose style showed the way.

Desk Rider

Shining,
poised on needle feet
upon a hard chrome plain,
the wire cowboy
rides his wiry horse,
endless rocking,
ever hopeful in his search
across the teak-grain vista
of my desk.

Passage

Passage
caused by yearning
births a restless journey
about the globe in sea salt moved
suspended and transmuted for the ride
on swells of moon-and-sun-brought tides
to kiss a shore and stay
with one who feels
passage

Last Stroll

*H*ow many walks we've taken!
scented life our joyous thread
along the gravel pathways
to some resting place ahead.

Will you walk me to my grave?
speak sweet words to me today?
Will you think of who we are
as you carry me away?

Again I sense your caring--
I can feel it as I sway;
how I thank you for your gift
as you grieve with me this way.

Tattoo, tattoo, the rhythms
of our time that sings so bright,
echo in this place I greet
in peace for eternal night.

For Ambrose

*I*n the Midst of Life:
Lift his cover and take note,
An occurrence there.

Purity and Worth

Sterling
values tested
for purity and worth
as moonlight grades its silver glow
and sunshine ranks its golden light on plants
through Yin and Yang's veracity
displayed in chlorophyll
virtue beyond
sterling

Tickle Time

Sunday
captures my soul
and bathes it in bubbles
that burst and tickle a fancy
day off

Part II
MORE REASON

The Tavern of My Delight Serves No Beer

*T*he tavern of my delight serves no beer;
no booze, no drugs, no artificial highs,
just ambience of light and laughter, cheer.

The tavern has no name, no place; but here
when eventide falls, senses amplified,
the tavern of my delight serves no beer.

Allegro beats my heart when you appear,
gentle one for whom words rarely apply,
just ambience of light and laughter, cheer.

No walls serve the tavern when you are near,
silvery Yin--goddess-light satisfies;
the tavern of my delight serves no beer.

We dance to a romantic balladeer's
view of life, multicolored butterflies,
just ambience of light and laughter, cheer.

Now transfixed on the terraced belvedere,
breathless, the, moonlit sea bids me sigh--
the tavern of my delight serves no beer
just ambience of light and laughter, cheer.

Muffin Trouble

Muffins
have a habit
of being on my plate
when I don't want them to be there
because they are so good and I am not
and the cook has no sympathy
for my sensed addiction
to sniff and eat
muffins

The Look of Oak

Oak trees
delight my soul
with their tough gnarly limbs
clad in green for spring and summer
show their maturity in dusty grays
to later crinkle in dry air
before autumn wind huffs
and bares the staid
oak trees

Summer Deal

Water
makes sublime clouds
when conditions are right
only to collect as droplets
that fall and splatter on my fresh-washed car
to dry as so many measles
that demand attention
from hard streams of
water

Gray as Gloaming in Winter

*E*gad, what a horse with his eyes alight!
His coat a rich gray, his white flecks, ablaze—
the tones of a crisp snowy day, this sight!

A fog starts to rise and he moves through a haze
to pose in a light, wispy shroud; he stands
for us, as with art on a wall, appraised.

Extinct are his eyes save for clues barely scanned;
aspects we see blink and disappear—
obscured in the brume, fuzzy dusk at hand.

Missouri Tiger Lily Time

*S*late clouds scud southward
lampoon meadow lifts and falls
barely high enough
above to keep brave tigers
bright and free of foggy coats

Good Company

*F*inding trills in vacuum,
like reading blank pages
beautifully bound,
leaves the lark singing
endlessly
in a place it will never be,
its passion silenced.

Would that I find
the wonderful bird's song
amidst the full roar of life
singing its heart out--
my ears seek the spill
of touched life
that gives the song its worth

The Other Stuff

*D*amned if it didn't happen to me.
It's been a time coming, I admit,
and friends have warned me—
more than once—that it would:

Those busses, the stations,
just rabbit-warren rides
on raceways for snails
through towns crawling with crooks.
You bounce and jiggle with folks
you don't know. Hell, they stuff you
so close your clothes get pressed
for free. But pickpockets have timing and knack.
They're so smooth. We know. You'll see.

So I "saw", this morning. And Poof!
No more phone. I didn't feel a thing.
But I'm ready now and "on" again
thanks to *Phones on the Go*...just
waiting for Jen's pleasant call.

Be more careful? You can bet.
Manãna, when the commute bus rolls.
Right now, I'm tired, and so close
to my rolling sanctuary home—
its stillness, its leather, anodyne.
This madness can wait outside!

Still, the theft lends one answer to
the question some ask
how bums have stuff and don't worry?
There's more of us here to rob!
Okay, too much, but
I'm still bummed enough to gripe.
Take the one fussing with a cell by
the news stand—The news stand!
I should thank him for that,
misguided sentinel that he is:
I can fulfill my promise of
a paper for Jen.

I dig past cash in a clip, for coins,
insert them, lift the lid and…wham-o!
I'm jarred.
It's the bum, and he's flustered.
Sorry mister! the gravelly voice grinds
while his thick calluses swipe at my clothes.

I check my pockets so fast! It's there.
He looks hurt: *What a zoo!*
I nod as nausea attacks. *It sure is!*
I tuck away the paper as he spins and
accelerates toward a bus.

His is a deft slide
into the wavering human turf.
How does he afford the ride, poor guy?

I get to the car, slip inside, settle low,
let its peace work on my nerves.
The sunset outside kindles a glow and
I tap a last call for Jen's needs.
The paper? Done deal.
Some milk? Okay.

Then I think of the bum and his plight,
the phone I still have as I drive.
I'm happy enough.
One theft is enough for the day.

But no, I learn at the store,
the clip is gone, along with
its hard-won bills.
I smile without joy and
dig for a card to pay for milk
Jen needs for the pie.

On reflection though, the filth,
the torn and smeared clothes,
the unshaved yellow beard,
are not what return, what I rue.
It's the furrow of concern he pasted
on his dirty brow, that and
the mock pain revealed through
a set of very clear eyes.

Hold My Hand

Harry William Hunt (1923-2009). Medium: painted and stained wood (1x2), hand crafted and lettered.

Questions, Questions

How old are you, sir?
I'm older than life that runs and jumps,
younger than death
that moves when kicked.

Are you foolish, sir?
More than a surgeon cutting to heal,
Less than a clown
at a funeral.

What makes you happy, sir?
The rhythms, the noise as we shape our
days; colors and textures
of a sensory kind.

Are you ever angry, sir?
Often, lad, about many things I let
steep into passion,
then free by work shaped
by its inspiration.

I have so many questions, sir!
Long may you ask them,
let your list grow long;
see the cat paw the water-glass,
learn why she yowls her song.

Part III
MOSTLY LOVE

The Stuff of Us

An inviting time with you beside a canal
passes with our feet dangling from
an ancient stone wall.

Hungry, eager ducks below your toes
rasp demands for the bread you drop,
blithe tumbling crumbs that glance

from your sun-warmed knees,
down onto glistening backs, and
into upturned, chattering beaks.

Clever webbed feet paddle in concert
on teal-hued, shifting currents—
imperfect circles maneuvered

to keep sight of your priceless,
dwindling trove.
You click sandaled heels and

shake out the bag,
crumple it into a useless brown ball.
The store is clearly closed

yet the message falls
as a feather on granite
in a place where no one cares.

You glance my way with twinkling eyes,
knight me with a beguiling smile, then
we rise on the verge of night.

Our feet still play crunchy duets
as we step on crinoline leaves,
but their rhythms slow as

The canal drifts away, as
we nuzzle and shift beneath
the sparkling star-blanket, ambling home.

Time Travel: A Western Solution

Lasso Time! Wrest its moves from round the pen—
step aboard to tame the beast, at least to
set its corkscrew straight, guide its headlong plunge ...
Just pick a foxtrot, waltz or boogie, and
plug it in your ears to accompany
spinning skies, cheering, concomitant crowds
who clap for other contestants seeded
in a mix that Time pays no mind to know ...
Lasso Time! Lope tethered through the gate for
parts unseen, or known, down the powdered road.

The *Magic* West of Home

Lubbers gape to know
what fate awaits the *Magic*
 as it pitches in seas
capped by brilliant spume—
wicked brine flicked
past a bow risen and smug,
to smack my waiting face.

I brace taught lines and sway,
then laugh in steely notes—
music to ape the overhead gray,
the shadow slayer battling the sun.

Man and nature twist,
heaving, crashing, straining—
life just laughing,
sailors free to set fine sails
with fullest love
against the roiling sea.

Snap, Crackle, Pique

*T*he bitter wind gives chase to win its prey,
to stop it in its tracks and turn it white,
to slow it to the season's inclination
to pause and fix what life has
overwrought, make sap to slow and
give a plant some peace, relax its
constant strife to reach for skies,
with trembling leaves in hallelujah dance,
its trunk, a consul's strength of warmth,
for tryst. We quake when caught and
quickly don our coats,
then blurt vile things about
the nasty quack who stole our heat
and took the joy away,
who makes us slide on water frozen flat.
A day or two or maybe more, it clicks:
sans pique, we feel the strident core of care.

Maggie's Trip

*I*f Maggie can leave so can anyone
with wheels and skill and a desire
to breathe air in other places.
But why should she make the trip

from all who care for her and
need her company at weddings and
funerals, back yard barbecues
and…anything, all the time?

Her presence stretches mouths
and grants eyes soft luster.
Maggie is light and now she wants
to brighten what we cannot see.

She will return. She says so
and I believe her because she
is Maggie and my heart knows
the truth of what she says—
it is in her eyes.

But the 'what ifs' freeze my heart
with their icy threats, even
as she quivers with delight
to leave and greet the choices.

The choices that bite and
tear and freeze and flame—
not to mention with laughter--
then claim her life forever.

Here are the keys, Maggie.
These start the sparkling car
with the new tires and the new
sound system, to melodize your miles

into your hoped-for future
filled with who knows what?
Keys shaped for the journey…
please make us one of your miles.

Prayer on the Wind

*H*ow many souls have passed Bodie's way
to plant a foot in the dirt,
to gaze and shiver at unheard cries,
of those whose feelings seem hurt?

A laugh and a shrug drive it away;
the town seems friendly enough
with silent mines and whispering winds
the spirits don't seem too gruff!

A zephyr screams and tugs at your sleeves,
your hat tries to leave your head;
you scan for trees but only see scrub
and markers of lasting stead.

Where are their lives, those who came and died?
Not in the dirt at your feet!
Their souls ply winds, it's where stories spin,
and in notes to loved ones, sweet.

Please grasp my sense, it is here I count,
here played my life's destiny.
Our goals were yours once, some of us stayed;
alone' screams our agony!

Auras remain as you jounce away—
mind views through poured window panes—
walls tell their tales down wrinkled, stained trails,
in halls that creak and complain!

Who needs to know the number of souls
with new names always to add?
Your heart is held by the fervent knell...
I'm here, come love me a tad!

Fusion

A hillside in fall

a stroll throughshowering leaves

small talk and laughter

to complete the ambience

set by a glance that stops time

Blink

There I was in the park

riding my bike before dinner and dark
when I found myself perched in a leafy gum tree
grinning like mad, at mom, you see,
who had drawn out her camera and pointed
quite straight, determined to snap the magic,
so great, when I slip into Cheshire Cat for none to see,
play tricks as I vanish...or remain truly me.

Flights of Fancy

Dipping
to feel the wind
ruffle your feathered wings
watching earth-sights loom to greet you
for joy

You fly
over green fields
dotted with live oak trees
places to flit and dodge boldly
below

Hungry
you land to eat
such things as you may find
then launch and wing another flight
for life

Above
you disappear
and now my mind must fly
to find you there in happiness
somewhere

My Place or Yours

A stroll

down foreign streets
feeling strange ambience
beneath thunderstorms that span time—
and place

Distortion

*M*y day for shadows

shapes the world in funny ways—
the long and the short

The Actor

I'm a sundial

I care nothing about time
just warmth as you pass

Moonless Muse

Here beneath the stars,
beneath a linen canopy,
heater-flames—so blue—
dip and sway that I may stay and
stare into the night—
moonless mysteries
for my muse to arrest on sight,
forms that float unbound
by docks and desks and walls with hooks—
celestial sprites that glide and slip,
freeze, compelling weary eyes
to dart about the enchanted skies,
bewitched, then close—oh, so fair—
till the chill slips through and
bids me to my late night lair.

Index of First Lines

Life with its gains,	6
First, the wind discovers chimes	8
I shiver when the moon sets,	9
He peeks at me, the golden eye, and grins,	9
The wind rustles trusting leaves to taunt me,	9
His eyes reveal, concern is real,	10
Dad looks hard to find his wooden mallet	10
The coffee percolated	10
Shining,	12
Passage	12
How many walks we've taken!	13
In the Midst of Life:	13
Sterling	14
Sunday	14
The tavern of my delight serves no beer;	16
Muffins	17
Oak trees	17
Water	17
Egad, what a horse with his eyes alight!	18
Slate clouds scud southward	18
Finding trills in vacuum,	19
Damned if it didn't happen to me.	19
The forest path traveled	22

How old are you, sir?	23
An inviting time with you beside a canal	25
Lasso Time! Wrest its moves from round the pen—	26
Lubbers gape to know	26
The bitter wind gives chase to win its prey,	27
If Maggie can leave so can anyone	28
How many souls have passed Bodie's way	29
A hillside in fall	30
There I was in the park	30
Dipping	31
A stroll	32
My day for shadows	32
I'm a sundial	32
Here beneath the stars,	33

A native of California, a graduate of Missouri State University, and a globe trotting student of mankind, Jim has taken myriad inspirations and applied them to novels (*Sport of Hearts*, *Kid Me You Die*), won a Writer's International Network Award for his short story, *Sparkling Water, Twinkling Eyes*, and is currently developing a television pilot.